For the *Love* of the

Buckeyes

An A-to-Z
Primer for
Buckeye Fans of
All Ages

Foreword by Archie Griffin

Written by Frederick C. Klein   Illustrations by Mark Anderson

When Ohio State hired Jim Tressel as football coach in 2001, I could see his character, his personality, his integrity, the way he shapes young men's lives—not only on the football field but, more importantly, off it—and I knew we had the right man to lead our team, our community, and our fans to where they wanted to be. I was totally confident that the Buckeyes were in great hands.

At the end of coach Tressel's second season, on January 3, 2003—a night I will never forget—the Buckeye nation was well represented at the Fiesta Bowl, where Ohio State was playing Miami for the national title. You looked around the stadium and saw nothing but scarlet and gray. I shouldn't have been surprised by the effort our fans made to be there. We had 16,000 tickets to sell, but somehow, some way, our fans managed to get more. I was blown away by how loyal our Ohio State fans are.

At the end of the night, after coach Tressel accepted the national championship trophy, I was left with one thought: Ohio State is a special place because of special people. It has been led by extraordinary individuals through its history. In this book, you will read about some of the wonderful folks who made us what we are, and about what they have done for football—something that is in our blood in this great state.

—Archie Griffin

"A" is for

The Assassin;

For Tatum, it fit.
When he hit a ball carrier
The poor guy stayed hit.

Jack Tatum was recruited as a running back but was switched to cornerback his first year of college. He stayed there and earned a reputation as one of the hardest tacklers ever to play the position. He started on the Buckeyes' national-champion 1968 team and was a consensus All-Amercan in 1969 and 1970. His teams won 27 of their 29 games in his three seasons in Columbus. He later starred for the Oakland Raiders of the National Football League.

"B" is for

Buckeye Grove,

Also for The Band.
When it comes to tradition
The Bucks lead the land.

Ohio State football is encased in a rich patina of lore. Buckeye Grove near Ohio Stadium, begun in 1934, contains a buckeye tree planted in honor of each OSU player who achieves first-team All-American status. Players run through the Tunnel of Pride, formed by former players, in each home game against Michigan, and receive a charm depicting a pair of gold football pants if they win that big annual game. The list goes on. The Buckeye Marching Band, 225-members strong, is famous for lending color and excitement to the gridiron spectacle.

"C" is for Cassady,

A lad who had "hop."
In the Fifties he led
His teams to the top.

Howard "Hopalong" Cassady, nicknamed for a popular Western-movie character, wasn't big (he stood 5'10" and weighed about 175 pounds) but was one of the quickest and most versatile backs ever to play for OSU. As a junior the Columbus native was the leading rusher, pass receiver, and kick returner on the 1954 national-championship team, and was an outstanding defensive back as well. He was even better the next year on his way to becoming a landslide winner of the Heisman Trophy, given to the season's outstanding collegiate player. When he graduated in 1955 he held OSU career records for rushing yardage (2,466), all-purpose yards (4,403), and scoring (222 points).

"D" is for Doss,

His game was defense;
His look was ferocious,
His manner intense.

Mike Doss, from Canton, Ohio, was a defensive back for the Buckeyes from 1999 through 2002. Equally adept at stopping the run and pass, he was a four-year starter at safety and a three-time All-American. One of his best games was his last—the 2003 Fiesta Bowl against Miami that made the Bucks national titleholders. There he made or assisted on nine tackles and his second-quarter pass interception and 35-yard runback set up his team's first touchdown in the 31–24 overtime win.

"E" is for Eddie,

Who ran tall and straight.
For the Bucks in '95,
He carried the freight.

At 6'3" Eddie George was tall for a modern-day tailback and his straight-up running style accentuated his height, but his 1995 season was the best for any OSU runner. He gained 100 yards or more rushing in 12 of his team's 13 games that year, including a one-game school record of 314 against Illinois; his season total of 1,927 yards is also a record. His efforts earned him the Heisman Trophy, the sixth for a Buckeye. He later had an excellent professional career with the Tennessee Titans.

"F" is for Fesler,

A do-everything guy.
As a player and coach
He hit the bull's eye.

Few college athletes have had careers equal to that of Wes Fesler at Ohio State. The Youngstown native was a three-time All-American in football (1928, 1929, and 1930), an All-American in basketball (1931), and a standout on the baseball team. His main position in football was end but he sometimes took to the backfield to run or pass for touchdowns. After graduation he went into coaching and worked as head football coach at Wesleyan, Pitt, Ohio State, and Minnesota, and head basketball coach at Harvard and Princeton. His 1949 OSU team was a Big Ten co-champion and beat California in the Rose Bowl.

"G" is for

Griffin,

That's Archie, first-name.
Two Heisman Trophies
Cemented his fame.

The first time he carried the ball for Ohio State, as a freshman in 1972, Archie Griffin fumbled and was removed from the game. Given another chance the next week against North Carolina the compactly built back ran for a then-school-record 239 yards, and his star was launched. He went on to set OSU marks for career rushing (5,589 yards) and all-purpose yards (6,559), and is the only player to win two Heisman Trophies (in 1974 and 1975). Later he became an assistant athletics director at the university and president of its alumni association.

"H" is for
Harley and Horvath,

Two true "triple threats."
With them Buckeye football
Was as good as it gets.

Charles "Chic" Harley was OSU's first nationally famous football star, a tailback who could run, pass, and kick with the best. In 1916 he led the Buckeyes to their first unbeaten and untied season and in 1919 sparked their first win over Michigan. Les Horvath played that same multitalent role in the early 1940s. His 1942 team went 9–1 and finished first in the Associated Press national-championship poll. In 1944 he recorded more than 1,200 all-purpose yards and became the first Buckeye winner of the Heisman Trophy.

"I" is the letter that gets the big dot.
For a Buckeye the honor cannot be forgot.

The Buckeye Marching Band first made its "Script Ohio" formation in 1936, and dotting the "i" became a highlighted ritual the next year. Usually the honor is given to a band member, but various notable Ohioans also have been singled out for such recognition. Among these have been Woody Hayes, the longtime Buckeye football coach, comedian Bob Hope, and golfing great Jack Nicklaus.

"J" is for Janowitz,

Who had lots of "go."
In '50 he carved
His name in the snow.

Vic Janowitz was another triple-threat tailback in the mold of Harley and Horvath, although he probably was a better punter and place-kicker than either of them. He won the 1950 Heisman Trophy despite his team's 6–3 won-lost record and second-place Big Ten finish. Ironically, he's best remembered for a game OSU lost—the November 25, 1950, "Snow Bowl" contest with Michigan, played in Columbus during a frigid blizzard. On a day when ball handling was nearly impossible, Janowitz supplied the only offensive score, a 38-yard field goal that was considered miraculous under the conditions. All of Michigan's points in the 9–3 outcome came on Buckeye turnovers. Janowitz punted 21 times that day, a school record that probably will never be broken.

"K" is for

Kern,

Who had a cool hand.
His '68 unit
Met every demand.

Rex Kern didn't have a powerful throwing arm, but his **short-passing accuracy and composure under fire** made him the perfect quarterback for the 1968 Buckeyes, Woody Hayes' best team. With other stars such as fullback Jim Otis, offensive-tackle Rufus Mayes, middle-guard Jim Stillwagon, and cornerback Jack Tatum, that squad completed its regular season with a 9–0 record and defeated an O.J. Simpson–led Southern California team in the Rose Bowl. Kern threw two touchdown passes and ran for 35 yards in that game, and was named the contest's Most Valuable Player.

"L" is for Linebacker,

The team set a high bar
With Spielman, Tom Cousineau,
And Randy Gradishar.

Powerful linebacking long has been a characteristic of Ohio State teams, and Chris Spielman, Tom Cousineau, and Randy Grandishar were among the best at the position. Spielman, from Massilon, played from 1984 through 1987 and is the school's all-time solo-tackles leader with 283. Cousineau (1975–1978), from Lakewood, and Gradishar (1971–73), from Champion, also rank high in many career defensive categories. All three players received first-team All-American mention after two of their collegiate seasons, and Gradishar was an Academic All-American to boot.

"M" is for Michigan,

Which all good Bucks despise.
A win over those guys is always a top prize.

Ohio State versus Michigan is one of the nation's premier college football rivalries: the annual November clash is a national television fixture, usually with bowl bids and poll rankings at stake. Michigan got off to a good start in the series, winning 13 of the first 15 games with two ties, but the Buckeyes have just about evened things since and the tally through 2007 had Michigan ahead, 57–41–6. In 2006, for the first time, the two teams met ranked No. 1 (OSU) and No. 2 (Michigan) nationally. Ohio State won a 42–39 thriller to capture the Big Ten title and the right to play in the Bowl Championship Series title game.

"N" is for Nugent,

He of the golden toe.
His kicks split the uprights, and brought woe to the foe.

Mike Nugent, from Centerville, was the most accurate and productive place-kicker in Ohio State history; when he graduated in 2004 he held or tied 22 school records, including the ones for most career points (356), most field goals (72), and highest field-goal percentage (.818). During a 2001–2002 span he kicked 24 field goals without a miss. In 2004 he won the Lou Groza Award as the nation's top collegiate place-kicker and became the only pure kicker to be named OSU's Most Valuable Player.

"O" is for

Ohio Stadium,

A "Shoe" that's always fit.
To visitors the place may seem
More like a big snake pit.

Ohio Stadium, called "The Horseshoe" or, simply, "The 'Shoe" because of its "U" shape, was opened in 1922 with a seating capacity of 66,210. It has been expanded several times and currently seats 102,329 people, making it one of the world's largest sporting venues. The Buckeyes' record there of 373–104–20 through 2007 attests to the enthusiastic home support the team receives.

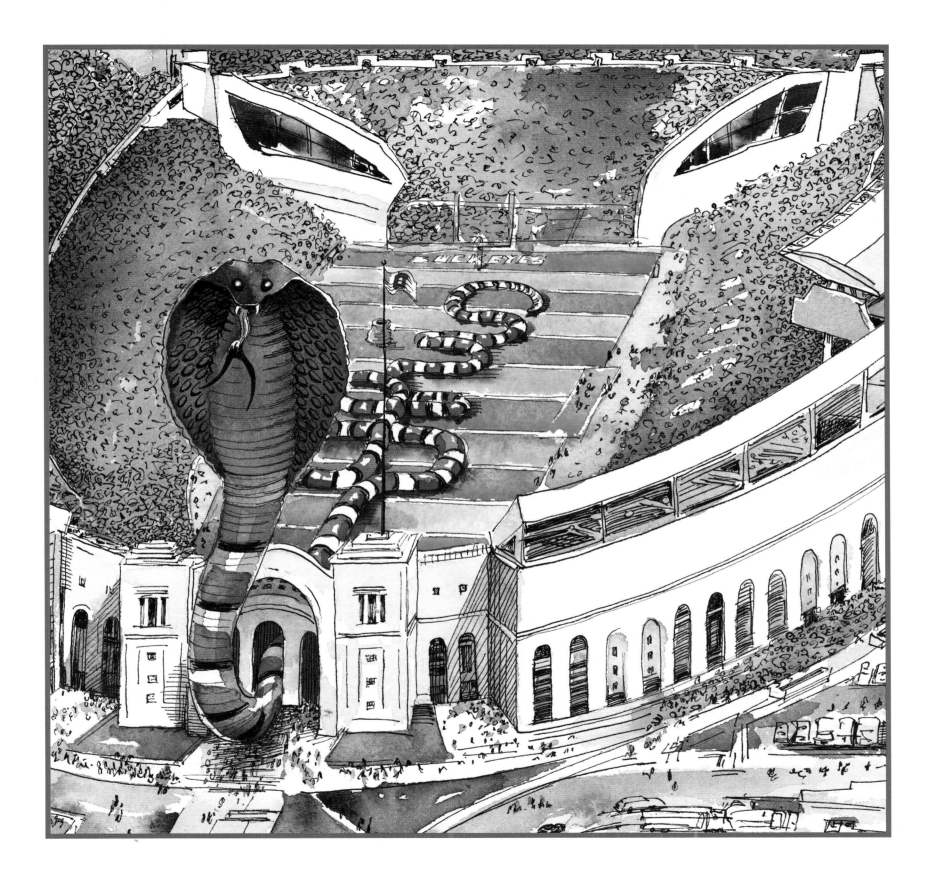

"P" is for
Parker
and Pace,

Those horses could plow.
Behind them Buck backs
Gained yardage—and how!

Jim Parker and Orlando Pace were two of the best offensive linemen ever. At OSU the broad-beamed Parker was a guard who made Woody Hayes' ground-based offense go during his 1954–1956 tenure. With the professional Baltimore Colts, Parker shifted to tackle and kept pass rushers away from Johnny Unitas during that team's glory years. Parker's plaques hang in both the college and NFL halls of fame. At 6'7" and 325 pounds, Orlando Pace is the prototypical current-day offensive tackle, a pass blocker without peer. At Ohio State he was a two-time All-American and won the 1996 Outland Trophy as the best college interior lineman. He later performed similarly with the NFL St. Louis Rams. He popularized the "pancake" block, where a blocker knocks a defender flat on his back.

"Q" is for the

Quest,

To climb the greasy pole.
For any Buckeye team
Number 1 is the goal.

"R" is for the Receivers–

Where should we begin?
How about Boston, Chris Carter,
Or, lately, Ted Ginn?

Ohio State stuck mostly to the ground in the Woody Hayes era, but more recently it has displayed potent passing attacks and top-flight receivers. Big, fast David Boston (1996–1998) is the school's all-time leader with 191 career receptions and 34 for touchdowns. Sure-handed Chris Carter (1984–1986) was a prime target in Columbus and later in the pros. The elusive Ted Ginn Jr. was Troy Smith's favorite passing option during the Buckeyes' excellent 2006 campaign.

"S" is for Smith_

Would he pass or run?
Foes couldn't decide so
He could do either one.

Troy Smith had a strong arm and the ability to scramble or run from a set play. This combination brought the 2006 Buckeyes to the national title game against Florida and Heisman Trophy and All-American honors to the Cleveland native. Smith's best performance that season was in the Big Ten championship showdown with Michigan, where he completed 29 of 41 passes for 316 yards and four touchdowns. The season before, he racked up 408 yards of total offense in leading OSU to a 34–20 win over Notre Dame in the Fiesta Bowl.

"T" is for

Tressel,

Whose whistle doth blow.
This quiet-looking gent
Runs the Buckeye show.

Jim Tressel lacks the sideline presence of some top college football coaches, but his calm, methodical approach to the game has reaped dividends in his seven seasons in Columbus. The son of a football coach, Tressel spent eight years as a collegiate assistant, including three at OSU (1983–1985), then built a Division I-AA powerhouse at Youngstown State that won four national titles over his 15 seasons there. His first Ohio State team, in 2001, went 7–5, but he's been a big winner since, capturing Big Ten crowns in 2002, 2005, and 2006 and a national championship in 2002. His older brother, Dick, is the Buckeyes' running back coach.

"U" is for Upset

In Tempe, AZ,
Where the Hurricanes fell and Buck fans sang with glee.

OSU came into the 2002 national championship game at the Fiesta Bowl in the Phoenix suburb of Tempe as an 11-point underdog to a top-rated Miami team that had swept all before it. The Bucks emerged with a 31–24, double-overtime victory that ranked among the best college games ever. The game was tied at 17 after regulation play. Miami scored a touchdown in the first overtime and the Bucks matched it after benefiting from a disputed pass-interference call. In the second OT Maurice Clarett scored on a 5-yard run and the Buck defense capped the win by stopping the mighty 'Canes on downs.

"V" is for the

Victory bell,

Which chimes out each win.
Its sound waves can rattle
Every pane in Franklin.

The 2,420-pound Victory Bell, a gift of the graduating classes of 1943, 1944, and 1945, sits 150-feet high in the southeast tower of Ohio Stadium. On a clear day its sound can be heard throughout Franklin County, of which Columbus is the seat.

"W" is for Woody,

Whose teams stirred the dust.
His motto was clear:
Victory is a must.

Wayne Woodrow "Woody" Hayes was the head football coach at Ohio State from 1951 through 1978, the longest span anyone has held that job. He was a hard-driving disciplinarian and a conservative strategist whose ground-based offense was characterized as "3 yards and a cloud of dust." His OSU teams compiled a 205–61–10 record, won five national championships (in 1954, 1957, 1961, 1968, and 1970), and won or shared 13 Big Ten crowns. Hayes often flashed a hot temper. He was fired after punching a Clemson player near the OSU bench during the 1978 Gator Bowl game. But while he asked much from his players he gave them much in leadership and loyalty, and is fondly remembered by many.

"X" is a

Mark

Coaches make in a book.
OSU has given plenty
Of those guys a look.

Ohio State has had numerous notable makers of X's and O's in addition to Tressel and Hayes. John Wilce (1913–1928) first gained national recognition for Buck teams. Francis Schmidt (1934–1940) was an offensive innovator. Paul Brown (1941–43) won a national title in Columbus (in 1942) before gaining even greater renown in the National Football League. Earle Bruce (1979–1987) and John Cooper (1988–2000) each won more than 70 percent of his games while head coach in Columbus and gathered Big Ten titles and high national ratings.

"Y" is for the

Years

When we attained dreams.
The Buck trophy cabinet
Bulges at the seams.

"Z" is for

Zarnas,

Rough and tough in the line,
But give him the ball
And he could do just fine.

Gustave Constantine Zarnas was born in Greece and came to the United States as a boy. He was a starting Buckeye guard from 1935 through 1937, an All-American his final year, and went on to play in the NFL. In a 1937 game against Indiana, at a time when the rules permitted linemen to handle the ball, he left his guard post, took a handoff from his quarterback, and threw a 57-yard touchdown pass.

Appendix

National Championships (7):

1942, 1954, 1957, 1961, 1968, 1970, 2002

Big Ten Championships, won or tied (31):

1916, 1917, 1920, 1935, 1939, 1942, 1944, 1949, 1954, 1955, 1957, 1961,
1968, 1969, 1970, 1972, 1973, 1974, 1975, 1976, 1977, 1979, 1981, 1984,
1986, 1993, 1996, 1998, 2002, 2005, 2006

Heisman Trophy (7):

Les Horvath (1944), Vic Janowitz (1950),
Howard Cassady (1955), Archie Griffin (1974 and 1975),
Eddie George (1995), Troy Smith (2006)

Outland Trophy (4):

Jim Parker (1956), Jim Stillwagon (1970),
John Hicks (1973), Orlando Pace (1996)

First-Team All-America selections: 168

Purchase high-quality 18x24 archival prints and T-shirts of your favorite Buckeye at:

Buckeyes
footballart.com

Special thanks to Susan and Jeff Cullen for sharing their time, knowledge, and Buckeye spirit.

Triumph Books
542 South Dearborn Street
Suite 750
Chicago, Illinois 60605
312. 939. 3330
Fax 312. 663. 3557

Printed in China
ISBN: 978–1–60078–137–7